I0017956

iPhone 15 PHONE GUIDE

Mastering the iPhone 15, Your Path to Seamless iOS Excellence

Brandon J. Price

All rights reserved. No part of this publication may be reproduced, distributed, or transmitted in any form or by any means, including photocopying, recording, or other electronic or mechanical methods, without the prior written permission of the publisher, except in the case of brief quotations embodied in critical reviews and certain other noncommercial uses permitted by copyright law.

Copyright © 2023.

Table of Contents

Introduction

Congratulations on your pick of the newest and most cutting-edge smartphone from Apple, the iPhone 15. This detailed guide is meant to help you unlock the full potential of your smartphone and make your iPhone 15 experience as pleasurable and productive as possible.

In this tutorial, we will take you on a tour through the different features and functions of the iPhone 15, from the basic setup to advanced tips and tricks. Whether you're new to the iPhone environment or a seasoned Apple user, there's something here for everyone.

We recognize that technology may often be scary, but fear not! We've designed this tutorial in a user-friendly manner, with clear and simple directions, useful pictures, and practical advice to aid you every step of the way.

Before we delve in, take the time to confirm your iPhone

15 is switched on and ready. Once you're set-up, let's explore the world of iOS 16 together and discover all the fantastic things your iPhone 15 can do. **Let's get started on this wonderful trip with your iPhone 15!**

Welcome to the iPhone 15

Welcome to the finest resource for mastering your iPhone 15! This guide is your route to unlocking the incredible potential of Apple's next flagship smartphone. Whether you're a beginner to the iPhone world or an established Apple devotee, this thorough guide is meant to enrich your iPhone 15 experience.

Our objective is to equip you with information, tips, and techniques that will help you get the most out of your iPhone 15. Inside these pages, you'll discover a wealth of knowledge that covers everything from the fundamentals of setup to the complex capabilities that make the iPhone 15 a genuine wonder of contemporary technology.

In a world where technology advances swiftly, we know that remaining up-to-date may be a problem. That's why we've designed this guide to give you clear, simple, and up-to-date information. We'll guide you through the essential functions of your iPhone 15 and expose you to fascinating new capabilities brought to life by iOS 16.

Before we go on this adventure together, make sure your iPhone 15 is ready to go. Charge it up, switch it on, and get ready to discover the extraordinary powers of your smartphone.

Without further ado, let's delve into the world of the iPhone 15 and learn how it may alter the way you communicate, work, and play. Welcome to an amazing trip with your iPhone 15!

Unboxing and Initial Setup

The time is here, and you're ready to begin your trip with the iPhone 15. Unboxing your new gadget is an exciting step, but let's make sure you do it correctly for a smooth start.

Unboxing Your iPhone 15:

Carefully open the container, taking note of any seals or tabs.

Lift the cover and behold your new iPhone 15.

Remove the gadget from its protective sleeve.

Checking the Contents: Besides your iPhone 15, you should find important accessories like earbuds, a charger, and a charging cable. Ensure that all products are present and undamaged.

Charging Your iPhone 15:

Connect the provided charger to a power source.

Plug the charging cord into the charger and the Lightning connector on your iPhone 15.

Allow your device to charge for a time, ensuring it has enough power to finish the setup procedure.

Powering On:

Press and hold the power button (usually placed on the right side of the device) until you see the Apple logo on the screen.

Follow the on-screen directions to pick your language and location.

Setting Up Wi-Fi and Cellular:

Connect to a Wi-Fi network by choosing one from the list and entering the password if needed.

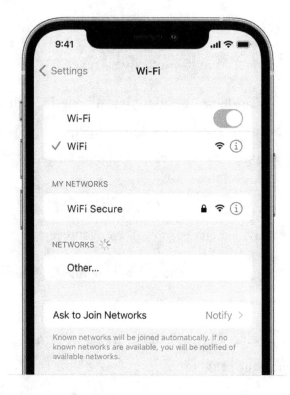

If you have a SIM card, place it into the SIM card tray (usually on the right side of the device) to enable cellular service.

Apple ID and iCloud:

Use your Apple ID to log in, or if you don't already have one, create one.

Choose whether to set up iCloud, which enables you to sync your data across devices.

Face ID/Touch ID Setup (Optional): Follow the on-screen steps to set up Face ID or Touch ID for greater security and convenience.

Restore from Backup (Optional): If you're upgrading from a prior iPhone, you may restore your data from an iCloud or iTunes backup.

Customize Your Settings: Personalize your smartphone by altering settings like display brightness, notifications, and sound preferences.

With your iPhone 15 unboxed and set up, you're now prepared to explore its various features and possibilities. In the next parts of this book, we'll go further into the functions that make the iPhone 15 a strong and flexible gadget.

Navigating iOS 16

iOS 16 is the throbbing heart of your iPhone 15, and learning how to navigate its interface will allow you to make the most of your device. Let's begin on a voyage via the smart iOS 16 interface:

The Home Screen: The Home Screen is where your applications reside. Simply press an app icon to open it. To view different pages from the Home Screen, swipe left or right. Use folders to organize programs by category or purpose.

Control Center: Swipe down from the top right corner (or up from the bottom, depending on your iPhone model) to reach the Control Center. Control Center enables easy access to critical settings including Wi-Fi, Bluetooth, screen brightness, and music controls.

Notifications: Swipe down from the top of the screen to access your Notifications. View and interact with alerts from applications here.

Multitasking: Swipe up from the bottom and pause in the middle to open the App Switcher. Here, you can view and switch between previously used applications.

Siri: Activate Siri by saying "Hey Siri" (if enabled) or by holding down the power button.

Siri can assist you in conducting chores, answering questions, and operating your device.

Search: Swipe down on the Home Screen to see the Search box. Use it to swiftly discover applications, contacts, and information on your smartphone.

Settings: The Settings app is where you can change your iPhone's settings and setups.

Organized into categories, you can customize anything from display settings to privacy and security.

App Store: The App Store is where you can find, download, and update applications.

Explore new applications, see reviews, and manage your downloads here.

Siri Suggestions: On the Home Screen, you'll discover Siri Suggestions and widgets that deliver app suggestions, pertinent information, and shortcuts based on your user habits.

AssistiveTouch (Optional): For individuals who prefer other navigation techniques, you may activate

AssistiveTouch in the Accessibility settings for extra control choices.

Gestures: iOS 16 depends on intuitive gestures. For instance, swiping motions replace the standard back button in many programs.

Accessibility Features: iOS 16 includes a broad variety of accessibility features to adapt to varied demands.

Explore these options under the Accessibility settings.

Navigating iOS 16 is a snap once you get comfortable with its gestures and features. As you proceed through this article, you'll get a greater grasp of iOS 16's capabilities and discover how to harness them to optimize your iPhone 15 experience.

Getting Started

Before you plunge into the rich world of your iPhone 15, it's vital to begin with the fundamentals. In this part, we'll lead you through the key procedures to set up your device, ensuring a smooth and trouble-free start.

Unboxing and Inspection: As we've discussed before, unbox your iPhone 15 carefully and check its contents to verify everything is there and in excellent shape.

Power On and Initial Setup: Press and hold the power button until the Apple logo displays to turn on your device. Follow the on-screen directions to pick your language and location.

Wi-Fi and Cellular Connection: Connect to a Wi-Fi network to facilitate quicker data transmission and smoother updates. If you have a SIM card, place it into the SIM card tray (usually found on the right side of the device) to enable cellular service.

Apple ID and iCloud: Sign in with your current Apple ID or create a new one if you don't have one. Your Apple ID is crucial for accessing the App Store, iCloud, and other Apple services. Decide if you wish to activate iCloud, which provides seamless syncing of your data across Apple devices.

Face ID/Touch ID Setup (Optional): For enhanced security and convenience, set up Face ID (if available) or Touch ID by following the on-screen instructions.

Passcode and Security: Create a secure passcode to safeguard your device and data. A strong passcode boosts your device's security.

Restore from Backup (Optional): If you're upgrading from a prior iPhone, you may restore your applications and data from an iCloud or iTunes backup.

Customize Your Settings: Personalize your iPhone 15 by modifying settings like display brightness, speaker preferences, and notification settings.

Apple Pay Setup (Optional): If you want to use Apple Pay, set it up by adding your credit or debit cards.

Screen Time and Parental Controls (Optional): If you have children using the device, you may set up Screen Time and parental controls to regulate app use and screen time limitations.

With these essential steps accomplished, your iPhone 15 is now ready to use. As you explore subsequent parts in this tutorial, you'll find how to maximize the potential of your smartphone, from fundamental communication tools to sophisticated productivity and entertainment choices. Welcome to the fascinating world of the iPhone 15!

Setting Up Your iPhone

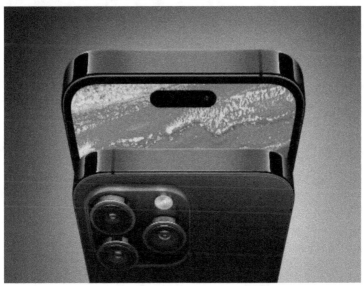

Setting up your iPhone 15 is a key initial step to ensure it functions effortlessly for your requirements. This section will walk you through the basic setup process, ensuring you get the most out of your gadget from the very beginning.

Activating Your Device: Power on your iPhone 15 by pressing and holding the power button until you see the Apple logo. Follow the on-screen directions to begin the setup procedure.

Select Your Language and Area: Choose your favorite language and the area or nation where you're situated.

Connect to a Wi-Fi Network: To accelerate the setup process and enjoy quicker internet rates, connect to a Wi-Fi network. Select your network and input the password if required.

Set Up Your Apple ID: Sign in with your current Apple ID if you have one. If not, start a new one. Your Apple ID is vital for accessing the App Store, iCloud, and other Apple services.

Face ID or Touch ID (Optional): Set up Face ID (if available) or Touch ID to increase the security and simplicity of unlocking your smartphone.

Create a Passcode: Establish a secure passcode for increased device security. A strong passcode is crucial to secure your data.

Restore from a Backup (Optional): If you're upgrading from a prior iPhone, you may select to restore your applications and data from an iCloud or iTunes backup.

Customize Your Settings: Personalize your iPhone 15 by adjusting settings like display brightness, sound preferences, and notification settings.

Set Up Apple Pay (Optional): If you want to utilize Apple Pay for easy payments, add your credit or debit cards at this step.

Enable Screen Time and Parental Controls (Optional): If you wish to regulate app use and establish screen time restrictions, consider setting Screen Time and parental controls.

Explore Accessibility Features (Optional): iOS provides a number of accessibility features to cater to varied demands. You may explore and customize these features under the Accessibility settings.

With these steps finished, your iPhone 15 is fully set up and ready to use. The following parts of this book will go further into certain features and functionalities, helping you to make the most of your new smartphone.

Welcome to the world of the iPhone 15!

Activating Your Device

Before you can plunge into the world of your iPhone 15, you need to activate it. Activation is a key step that guarantees your device is ready to use. This section will take you through the activation procedure.

Powering On Your iPhone 15: To begin, press and hold the power button found on the right side of your iPhone 15 until you see the Apple logo on the screen. This means that your gadget is turning on.

Welcome Screen: After a few seconds, you'll be welcomed with the "Hello" screen in several languages. Swipe up from the bottom of the screen or tap the "Home" button (if your device has one) to get started.

Language and location Selection: You'll be requested to pick your favorite language and location. Choose the language you're most familiar with, then choose your present location or nation.

Connect to a Wi-Fi Network: To begin, you'll need to connect your iPhone 15 to a Wi-Fi network. This facilitates speedier data transmission and a smoother setup procedure. Select your Wi-Fi network from the list and input the password if needed.

Cellular Setup (if applicable): If your iPhone 15 allows cellular connection and you have a SIM card, place it into the SIM card tray (usually found on the right side of the device). Follow the on-screen directions to finish the cellular activation procedure.

Activating using Apple ID: If you have an Apple ID, sign in with it at this point. Your Apple ID is crucial for accessing the App Store, iCloud, and other Apple services. If you don't have an Apple ID, you may create one at this stage.

Face ID or Touch ID Setup (Optional): Depending on your iPhone 15 model, you may be requested to set up Face ID or Touch ID for enhanced security and convenience. Follow the on-screen directions to finish this procedure.

Establish a Passcode: To safeguard your device and data, establish a secure passcode. It's advisable to choose a passcode that is not readily guessable.

Restore from a Backup (Optional): If you're upgrading from a prior iPhone, you may select to restore your applications and data from an iCloud or iTunes backup.

Customize Settings: Personalize your iPhone 15 by adjusting settings like display brightness, sound preferences, and notification settings.

With these procedures finished, your iPhone 15 is now activated and ready to use. You've successfully completed the first setup step, and you're ready to explore the device's features and functions.

Apple ID and iCloud

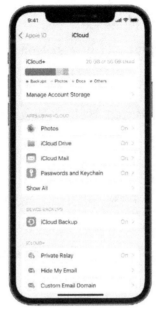

Your Apple ID and iCloud account are the keys to unlocking the full potential of your iPhone 15. In this part, we'll look into the relevance of your Apple ID and how iCloud may improve your iPhone experience.

What is an Apple ID?

Your Apple ID is a unique identity that enables you to access different Apple services, including the App Store, iTunes, iCloud, iMessage, and FaceTime. It's vital for a smooth Apple ecosystem experience.

Creating or Signing in with Your Apple ID: If you already have an Apple ID, sign in with it during the first setup of your iPhone 15. If you don't have an Apple ID, you may create one by choosing the "Create Apple ID" option. Follow the on-screen steps, give your information, and select a secure password.

iCloud: Your Cloud-Based Hub: iCloud is Apple's cloud-based storage and syncing service. It keeps your images, movies, documents, applications, and more in sync across all your Apple devices. When setting up your iPhone 15, you'll have the choice to activate iCloud. Doing so enables you to effortlessly access your data from wherever, as long as you're connected to the internet.

Key iCloud Features:

iCloud Images: Store and access your images and videos across all your devices. Changes you make to your picture collection on one device are mirrored on others.

iCloud Drive: Safely save your papers and files in iCloud, making them available from your iPhone, iPad, Mac, or PC.

Find My iPhone: iCloud allows the Find My iPhone function, which lets you find your smartphone if it's lost or stolen.

iCloud Backup: Automatically back up your smartphone to iCloud, ensuring your data is secure and can be recovered if required.

iCloud Keychain: Securely store and sync your passwords and payment information across your devices for convenient access.

Managing iCloud Storage: Your Apple ID comes with a limited quantity of free iCloud storage (5GB). Depending on your demands, you may need to manage your iCloud storage by subscribing to a higher plan if you surpass this limit.

Privacy and Security: Apple takes your privacy and security seriously. iCloud data is protected, and you have control over what is backed up and synced to the cloud.

Family Sharing (Optional): iCloud lets you set up Family Sharing, where you may share bought applications, media, and more with family members. This is a terrific method to keep your family connected and organized.

By knowing the purpose of your Apple ID and the

possibilities of iCloud, you'll be better able to manage your data and enjoy a smooth, linked experience across all your Apple devices.

Essential Features

Your iPhone 15 is loaded with several critical features that make it a flexible and powerful gadget. In this part, we'll cover these fundamental functions to help you get the most out of your iPhone 15.

Making Calls and Sending Messages: Your iPhone 15 is, at its heart, a communication device. Use the Phone app to make calls and the Messages app to send text messages and multimedia communications.

Internet and Connectivity: Connect to the internet via Wi-Fi or cellular data. Use Bluetooth for wireless accessories and AirDrop for exchanging files with adjacent Apple devices.

Using Siri and Voice Control: Activate Siri by voice command or by pushing and holding the power button.

Siri can execute jobs, answer inquiries, and operate your device.

Contacts & Address Book: Manage your contacts with the Contacts app. Sync your contacts with your Apple ID to keep them constant across your devices.

Email and Calendar: Set up and utilize the Mail app to handle your emails. Stay organized with the Calendar app to plan events, appointments, and reminders.

Safari Web Browser: Safari is your entrance to the internet. Use it to explore websites, save your favorite pages, and open several tabs for efficient online browsing.

App Store and Downloads: Access the App Store to explore and download a large assortment of applications. Keep your applications updated to benefit from the newest features and security updates.

Privacy and Security: Configure privacy settings, app permissions, and security features to keep your device and data secure.

Accessibility Features: iOS has a broad variety of accessibility features to satisfy varied demands, such as VoiceOver for the visually impaired and Magnifier for zooming in on items.

Battery Optimization: Manage your battery life by altering settings, such as screen brightness and background app refresh.

System upgrades and Maintenance: Stay up to date with the latest iOS upgrades to guarantee your device functions smoothly and securely. Regularly backup your iPhone to iCloud or your PC.

Troubleshooting and FAQs: Familiarize yourself with frequent difficulties and their remedies. Knowing how to troubleshoot issues may save you time and stress.

Voice and Video Calls: Utilize FaceTime and other voice and video call programs to keep connected with friends and family, even when they're miles away.

Messages and Multimedia: Explore the various capabilities of the Messages app, including sending photographs, videos, stickers, and utilizing the Animoji/Emoji feature.

Notifications and Do Not Disturb: Manage notifications to control which applications may disturb you. Use Do Not Disturb to stop alerts at certain times.

These vital elements form the core of your iPhone 15's usefulness. As you explore further into your iPhone's capabilities, you'll learn how these essential functions may be utilized to improve your communication, work, and entertainment experiences.

Making Calls and Sending Messages

Your iPhone 15 is a strong communication tool that lets you interact with people via calls and messaging. In this part, we'll learn how to make calls and send different sorts of messages using your iPhone.

Making Phone Calls:

Using the Phone App: Locate and touch the "Phone" app on your Home Screen.

Dialing a Number: To call someone, hit the keypad symbol in the bottom menu, input the phone number, and then click the green call button.

Contacts: Alternatively, touch the "Contacts" tab to discover and call someone from your stored contacts.

Recent Calls: Access your call history by pressing the "Recents" tab.

Answering Calls: When someone calls you, you'll see their name or number on the screen. Swipe right to respond or swipe left to refuse. You may also hit the volume keys to quiet an incoming call or click the power button to send the call to voicemail.

Sending Text Messages (SMS):

Using the Messages App: Locate and touch the "Messages" app on your Home Screen.

Creating a New Message: Tap the compose icon (typically a pencil or paper and pen) to start a new message.

Recipient: Enter the recipient's name or phone number in the "To:" area.

Type Your Message: Tap the text area at the bottom and start typing your message.

Sending: Tap the blue send button (usually a paper aircraft symbol) to send your message.

Sending Multimedia Messages (MMS):

Photographs and Videos: In the Messages app, you can send photographs and videos by pressing the camera icon next to the text box.

GIFs and Stickers: You may also incorporate GIFs, stickers, and other multimedia components to make your communications more expressive.

iMessage (Apple Devices Only): If the receiver also uses an Apple device, your messages may be transmitted as iMessage, which provides extra capabilities like reading receipts, typing indications, and the option to send higher-quality photographs and videos.

Group conversations: You may create and participate in group conversations by adding numerous receivers to a message thread.

Other Messaging Programs: Besides the Messages app, you may explore third-party messaging programs accessible in the App Store, such as WhatsApp, Facebook Messenger, and Telegram.

FaceTime (Video and Audio chats): For video and audio chats with other Apple users, you may utilize the FaceTime app. Simply open it, choose a contact, and choose whether to initiate a video or voice call.

Voicemail: Missed calls typically lead to voicemail messages. Access your voicemail by touching the "Voicemail" tab in the Phone app.

These key communication functions of your iPhone 15 will help you remain connected with friends, family, and coworkers. Whether you're conducting conventional phone conversations or sending advanced multimedia messaging, the iPhone 15 has you covered.

Internet and Connectivity

Your iPhone 15 gives effortless access to the internet and a broad variety of connection possibilities. In this part, we'll study how to connect to the internet, manage your connections, and use different connectivity capabilities.

Wi-Fi Connection:

Connecting to Wi-Fi: To connect to a Wi-Fi network, go to "Settings" > "Wi-Fi," and pick your chosen network. Enter the password if necessary.

Auto-Join Networks: Enable "Auto-Join" to automatically join recognized Wi-Fi networks when in range.

Cellular Data:

Cellular Network: If you have a SIM card and cellular plan, your iPhone 15 can access the internet through cellular data. Ensure cellular data is enabled in "Settings"

> "Cellular."

Bluetooth Connectivity:

Pairing Devices: Use Bluetooth to link your iPhone with wireless devices like headphones, speakers, and keyboards. Go to "Settings" > "Bluetooth" to commence pairing.

AirDrop:

Sharing Files: AirDrop enables you to share images, movies, documents, and more with nearby Apple devices. Access it through the Control Center or share options inside applications.

VPN (Virtual Private Network):

Enhanced Privacy: Set up a VPN under "Settings" > "VPN" to encrypt your internet connection and boost online privacy and security.

Personal Hotspot:

Sharing Your Data: Turn on the Personal Hotspot option to share your iPhone's internet connection with other devices, such as laptops and tablets.

Airplane Mode:

Flight-Friendly: Use Airplane Mode while flying to disable all wireless features, ensuring your smartphone conforms with airline laws.

Ethernet (with Adapter):

Wired Connection: If required, you may connect to the internet through Ethernet using a suitable adaptor.

AssistiveTouch (Optional):

Accessibility Navigation: AssistiveTouch may aid users with physical difficulties in navigating the device and managing connection functions.

Internet Tethering:

Sharing Mobile Data: Use internet tethering to share your iPhone's cellular data connection with other devices through USB, Bluetooth, or Wi-Fi.

VPN & Privacy Settings:

Protecting Your Data: Configure VPN and privacy settings to shield your online activity and personal information.

Mobile Data Usage:

Data Management: Monitor your mobile data consumption in "Settings" > "Cellular" to minimize overage costs.

Roaming:

International go: If you go overseas, be careful of roaming costs. Consider obtaining an overseas plan or utilizing local SIM cards.

By mastering these internet and connection functions on your iPhone 15, you'll be able to remain connected, browse the web, and share material conveniently, both at home and on the move. Whether you're surfing the web, streaming entertainment, or interacting with others, your iPhone 15 offers the tools you need for a connected experience.

Wi-Fi and Cellular Data

Wi-Fi and cellular data are the lifelines of your iPhone 15, offering internet access everywhere you go. In this part, we'll discuss how to manage and make the most of your Wi-Fi and cellular connections.

Connecting to Wi-Fi:

Accessing Wi-Fi Settings: Open "Settings" and touch "Wi-Fi."

Selecting a Network: Choose your chosen Wi-Fi network from the list.

Password: If necessary, provide the network password.

Auto-Join: Enable "Auto-Join" to automatically join recognized Wi-Fi networks when in range.

Cellular Data Usage:

Monitoring Data use: Keep track of your cellular data use under "Settings" > "Cellular."

Cellular Data restriction: Set a data use restriction or warning to prevent exceeding your plan's limitations.

Wi-Fi Assist:

Seamless Transition: Wi-Fi Assist enables your iPhone to access cellular data when the Wi-Fi connection is poor.

Enable it under "Settings" > "Cellular" > "Wi-Fi Assist." **Personal Hotspot:**

Sharing Data: Use a Personal Hotspot to share your iPhone's cellular data connection with other devices.

Activation: Find this function in "Settings" > "Personal Hotspot."

Wi-Fi Calling:

Enhanced Calling: Enable Wi-Fi Calling in "Settings" > "Phone" > "Wi-Fi Calling" to make calls via Wi-Fi when your cellular connection is poor.

Reset Network Settings:

Troubleshooting: If you find connection troubles, try resetting network settings in "Settings" > "General" > "Reset."

VPN Configuration:

Privacy and Security: Configure a VPN (Virtual Private Network) under "Settings" > "VPN" to increase online privacy and security.

Roaming (If Traveling):

International Travel: When traveling overseas, be careful of data roaming rates. Consider an international plan or utilizing local SIM cards.

Low Data Mode:

Data Conservation: Enable "Low Data Mode" in "Settings" > "Cellular" to limit data use in the background.

Carrier Settings Updates:

Automatic Updates: Carrier settings updates may be available. Allow automatic updates under "Settings" >

"General" > "About."

AssistiveTouch (Optional):

Accessibility Navigation: AssistiveTouch can assist users with physical limitations in controlling Wi-Fi and cellular settings.

By mastering these Wi-Fi and cellular data management capabilities on your iPhone 15, you can remain connected wherever you are while properly monitoring your data use.

Bluetooth and AirDrop

Bluetooth and AirDrop are flexible connection tools that increase your iPhone 15's possibilities for wireless communication and file sharing. In this part, we'll cover how to utilize Bluetooth for connecting accessories and how to exchange files easily via AirDrop.

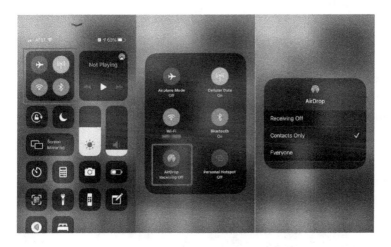

Bluetooth Connectivity:

Accessing Bluetooth Settings: Open "Settings" and hit "Bluetooth."

Turning Bluetooth on/off: Toggle the Bluetooth switch to turn it on or off.

Pairing Bluetooth Accessories:

Pairing Process: To connect Bluetooth peripherals, such as headphones, speakers, or keyboards, follow these basic steps:

Enable Bluetooth on your iPhone 15.

Turn on the accessory's pairing mode (see the accessory's handbook).

In the Bluetooth settings, choose the attachment from the list of accessible devices.

Follow any on-screen instructions to finish the pairing procedure.

Managing Paired Devices:

Connected Devices: Under Bluetooth settings, you may view a list of associated devices. Tap on a device to connect or detach it.

Bluetooth Settings:

Rename Device: You may personalize the name of your iPhone for simple identification in Bluetooth settings.

Forget This Device: If required, you may forget a linked device to remove it from your list.

AirDrop for File Sharing:

Accessing AirDrop: Open Control Center by swiping down from the top right (or up from the bottom, depending on your iPhone model). Long-press the connection section (top left).

AirDrop Settings: Customize your AirDrop settings to enable receiving from "Contacts Only" or "Everyone."

Sharing Files: To transfer files using AirDrop, follow these steps:

Open the file or material you wish to share (e.g., a picture, document, or website).

Tap the Share button (typically represented by a square with an arrow pointing up).

From the share sheet, choose the recipient's device name when it appears in the AirDrop area.

The receiver will get a notice and may choose to accept or deny the file.

Receiving AirDrop Files:

Accepting Files: When someone gives you an AirDrop file, you'll get a notice. Tap "Accept" to store the file on your smartphone.

AirDrop Compatibility:

Apple Ecosystem: AirDrop works effortlessly across Apple devices, such as iPhones, iPads, and Macs. It provides quick and secure file transfers.

Troubleshooting:

AirDrop Not Working: If AirDrop experiences troubles, check Bluetooth and Wi-Fi are active, and both devices are in close vicinity with AirDrop enabled.

AssistiveTouch (Optional):

Accessibility Navigation: AssistiveTouch may aid users with physical limitations in controlling Bluetooth and AirDrop settings.

By learning how to utilize Bluetooth for accessory pairing and AirDrop for fast and seamless file sharing, you'll get the most of your iPhone 15's wireless capabilities, whether you're connecting to headphones or emailing files to friends and coworkers.

Using Siri and Voice Control

Siri and Voice Control are strong voice-activated capabilities on your iPhone 15 that enable you to communicate with your smartphone, do tasks, and acquire information hands-free. In this part, we'll discuss how to utilize Siri and Voice Control successfully.

Activating Siri:

Voice Command: Say "Hey Siri" to activate Siri when your smartphone is connected to power or use the side button (on later iPhone models) or the home button (on older models).

Interacting with Siri:

Voice Commands: Once Siri is active, deliver your order or inquiry clearly and naturally.

Examples: You may ask Siri to perform many things, including setting reminders, sending messages, making calls, and answering inquiries.

Common Siri Commands:

"Send a message to [Contact Name]."

"Call [Contact Name]."

"Set a timer for 10 minutes."

"Play [Song/Artist/Album] on Apple Music."

"What's the weather today?"

"Translate 'hi' to French."

"Remind me to purchase groceries at 5 PM."

"Open [App Name]."

Customizing Siri:

Personal Information: You can train Siri to recognize your voice and understand your preferences better.

Settings: Configure Siri's behavior and voice under

"Settings" > "Siri & Search." **Voice Control:**

Enabling Voice operation: Voice Control enables you to operate your device using voice commands. Enable it in "Settings" > "Accessibility" > "Voice

Control."

Using Voice Control:

Commands: You can execute numerous actions using Voice Control, including launching applications, navigating menus, and inputting text.

Example Commands:

"Open Messages."

"Scroll down."

"Tap Home."

"Go to Settings."

Voice Control Customization:

Custom Commands: You may build custom commands for Voice Control to execute particular operations or launch applications not recognized by default.

Accessibility Features:

Accessibility Shortcut: Triple-press the side button (on newer models) or the home button (on older models) to rapidly activate Voice Control or other accessibility capabilities.

Privacy Considerations:

Privacy: Siri and Voice Control are meant to protect your privacy. You may examine and erase your voice interactions with Siri under "Settings" > "Privacy" >

"Analytics & Improvements."

Troubleshooting:

Improving Accuracy: If Siri or Voice Control doesn't comprehend your orders adequately, try speaking more clearly or revising settings for improved recognition.

By learning Siri and Voice operate, you can do tasks, access information, and operate your iPhone 15 more effortlessly, whether you're driving, multitasking, or just prefer a hands-free connection with your device.

Voice Commands and Shortcuts

Your iPhone 15 enables you to utilize voice commands and shortcuts to expedite chores and automate procedures. In this part, we'll learn how to develop and utilize voice commands and shortcuts efficiently.

Siri Voice Commands:

Activation: Activate Siri by saying "Hey Siri" or holding down the side button (on later devices) or the home button (on older models).

Examples: Use Siri for voice-activated tasks, such as sending messages, setting reminders, making calls, and receiving information.

Creating Custom Siri Shortcuts:

Shortcuts App: Open the Shortcuts app (pre-installed on your iPhone) to build unique voice commands for certain tasks.

Creating Shortcuts: Follow these steps to create custom shortcuts:

Open the Shortcuts app.

Tap the "+" symbol to create a new shortcut.

Use the "Add Action" button to add actions to your shortcut. These actions may be a mix of system actions and third-party software activities.

Customize your shortcut's name and icon.

Save the shortcut.

Running Siri Shortcuts:

Using Voice: You may activate personalized Siri shortcuts by uttering the exact voice command you provided to them while Siri is enabled.

From Shortcuts App: You can also run custom shortcuts directly from the Shortcuts app by tapping on them.

Apple's Suggestions:

Siri Suggestions: Siri may suggest shortcuts based on your usage patterns and habits. You can activate these suggestions and create shortcuts from them.

Third-Party Shortcuts:

Integration: Many third-party apps support Siri Shortcuts. Check your favorite apps for shortcut integration and create voice-activated commands for those apps.

Automation:

Home App: If you have smart home devices, you can create automation in the Home app and use Siri to control your smart home with voice commands.

Personalized Shortcuts:

Contextual Shortcuts: Siri learns from your daily routines and can suggest personalized shortcuts based on your usage.

Managing Shortcuts:

Edit and Delete: You can edit or delete shortcuts at any time from the Shortcuts app.

Accessibility Features:

VoiceOver Support: VoiceOver, an accessibility feature, can read out your shortcuts and help users with visual impairments navigate them.

Troubleshooting:

Voice Recognition: For maximum results, talk properly while composing and utilizing voice commands and shortcuts.

App Compatibility: Ensure that third-party applications you wish to connect with Siri Shortcuts have the required rights and support.

By utilizing the power of voice commands and custom shortcuts, you can automate chores, retrieve information, and operate your iPhone 15 more effectively, making your device a customized and time-saving assistant suited to your requirements.

Productivity and Apps

Your iPhone 15 provides a broad choice of productivity applications and features that may help you keep organized, manage projects, and enhance your performance. In this part, we'll discuss some of the crucial productivity applications and strategies to get the most out of your iPhone.

Calendar:

Scheduling: Use the Calendar app to plan events, appointments, and reminders.

Syncing: Sync your calendar with other accounts, including iCloud, Google Calendar, or Microsoft Exchange, for smooth scheduling across devices.

Notes:

Note-Taking: The Notes app is perfect for scribbling down ideas, generating to-do lists, and keeping track of critical information.

Scanning: Use the built-in document scanner to digitize physical documents and store them as notes.

Reminders:

Task Management: Manage your tasks and to-do lists using the Reminders app.

Area-Based Reminders: Set reminders that activate when you arrive at or depart a certain area.

Files:

File Management: The Files app helps you to manage and access your files and documents saved locally and in cloud services like iCloud Drive, Google Drive, and Dropbox.

Apple Maps:

Navigation: Apple Maps lets you travel with

turn-by-turn instructions, real-time traffic updates, and public transit information.

Indoor Maps: Access indoor maps of malls and airports for easier navigation.

Safari Web Browser:

Web exploring: Safari is your preferred web browser for researching, shopping and exploring online.

Tab Management: Use tabbed browsing and Reader View for an orderly and distraction-free surfing experience.

Email:

Mail App: Manage your email accounts using the Mail app. While on the go, send and receive emails with ease.

Office and Productivity Apps:

Microsoft Office: Download programs like Word, Excel, and PowerPoint for document creation and editing.

Google Workspace: Access Google Docs, Sheets, and Slides for collaborative work.

Apple iWork: Use Pages, Numbers, and Keynote for creating documents, spreadsheets, and presentations.

Widgets:

Home Screen Widgets: Customize your Home Screen with widgets that provide at-a-glance information, such as weather, calendar events, and reminders.

Focus Mode:

Minimize Distractions: Use Focus mode to filter notifications and stay focused on tasks or activities that matter most.

Task Management Apps:

Third-Party Apps: Explore third-party task management apps like Todoist, Trello, and Asana for advanced project management and collaboration.

Password Managers:

Security: Consider using a password manager like 1Password or LastPass to securely store and autofill your passwords.

AssistiveTouch (Optional):

Accessibility Navigation: AssistiveTouch can assist users with physical disabilities in navigating productivity apps.

Shortcuts and Automation:

Streamline chores: Create shortcuts to automate common chores and save time. Integrate with productivity applications for even more efficiency.

By harnessing the capabilities of productivity apps and features on your iPhone 15, you can enhance your daily workflow, stay organized, and accomplish tasks more efficiently, whether you're working, studying, or managing your personal life.

Using Notes and Reminders

The Notes and Reminders apps on your iPhone 15 are essential tools for staying organized, jotting down important information, and managing tasks efficiently. In this section, we'll explore how to make the most of these apps.

Using the Notes App:

Creating Notes:

Go to your Home Screen and open the Notes app.

Tap the "+" button to make a new note.

Type or narrate your note using Siri.

Organizing Notes:

Create folders to classify your notes. Tap "Edit" in the Notes app, then "New Folder."

Use headers, bullets, and checklists to organize your notes.

Pin critical notes to the top of your list for easy access.

Multimedia Notes:

Add photographs, videos, doodles, and scanned documents to your notes.

Tap the camera or camera roll icon to connect multimedia.

Sharing Notes:

Collaborate with others by exchanging notes. Select "Add" after tapping the sharing button (an arrow-shaped box).

People" to invite others to contribute in real-time.

Use the "Send a Copy" option to send a message as a PDF or other formats.

Locked Notes:

Protect critical information by locking notes with a password, Face ID, or Touch ID.

Press the share sign and select "Lock Note" to lock a note.

Using the Reminders App:

Creating Tasks:

Open the Reminders app from your Home Screen.

Tap the "+" button to add a new task.

Enter the task specifics, such as due date and location.

Organizing Tasks:

Create lists to arrange similar tasks. To make a list, tap "New List".

Drag and drop tasks to rearrange them.

Use subtasks to break down complicated activities into smaller stages.

Notifications:

Reminders may deliver messages at certain times or places to help you recall things.

Set a due date, time, and location for each job.

Smart Lists:

The Reminders app features Smart Lists like "Today," "Scheduled," and "Flagged" to help you concentrate on activities that require urgent attention.

"Today" provides tasks with due dates for the current day.

Siri Integration: You may use Siri to generate and manage reminders. For example, say, "Hey Siri, remind me to purchase groceries at 5 PM." **Sharing Lists:**

Collaborate with others by sharing lists. Tap the share button and invite individuals to the list.

Shared lists enable multiple users to add, perform, and amend tasks.

Area-Based Reminders: Set reminders that activate when you arrive at or depart a certain area. This is excellent for activities like grocery lists.

By using the Notes and Reminders apps properly, you can keep track of critical information, manage projects, and remain organized in both your personal and business life with your iPhone 15.

Exploring the App Store

Exploring the App Store on your iPhone 15 is a terrific way to find and download a broad choice of applications that may improve your device's capabilities. Here's how to make the most of the App Store:

Opening the App Store:

Locate the App Store icon on your Home Screen (it looks like a blue "A").

Tap the icon to launch the App Store.

Navigating the App Store:

The App Store opens to the "Today" page by default, presenting highlighted applications and articles.

Explore the tabs at the bottom of the screen:

Today: Discover highlighted applications, articles, and app collections.

Games: Find and explore games available on the App

Store.

Applications: Browse and search for all sorts of applications, from productivity tools to leisure apps.

Updates: Check for updates to your installed applications.

Search: Use the search box to discover particular programs or explore categories.

Discovering Apps:

Scroll down on the "Today" page to view app collections, app of the day, and more.

Explore the "Apps" and "Games" sections to explore various categories and top rankings.

App Details:

Tap on an app's icon or name to visit its info page.

Here, you can read program descriptions, examine screenshots, check reviews, and see user ratings.

Downloading Apps:

To download an app, touch the "Get" button next to the app's name.

If the app is paid, you'll need to authenticate the purchase using Face ID, Touch ID, or your Apple ID password.

App Updates:

Regularly visit the "Updates" page to check for updates to your installed applications.

Tap "Update All" to update all applications or update them separately.

App Management:

Go to "options" > "App Store" to change options like automatic downloads and app ratings.

You may also adjust your Apple ID, payment methods, and subscriptions linked to the App Store.

App Search:

Use the "Search" option to locate certain applications by name or keywords.

Explore recommended search phrases for inspiration.

App Store Account:

To access your App Store account, touch your profile image in the upper right corner.

Here, you may access bought applications, and subscriptions, and redeem gift cards or discount coupons.

Family Sharing: If you have Family Sharing set up, you may share bought applications and subscriptions with family members.

want List: Add applications to your want list for future reference by touching the share icon on an app's information page and choosing "Add to Wish List."

Accessibility Features: The App Store is developed with accessibility in mind, making it usable for persons with impairments.

By browsing the App Store, you may discover and download applications that cater to your interests and requirements, whether it's for productivity, entertainment, health, or anything else you can think of. It's a massive digital marketplace where you can make your iPhone 15 uniquely yours.

Installing and Updating Apps

Installing and upgrading applications on your iPhone 15 is a basic procedure. Here's how to do it:

Installing Apps:

Open the App Store: Tap on the App Store icon on your Home Screen.

Browse or Search for an App:

To browse, explore the "Today," "Games," or

"applications" sections to find new applications and categories.

To search, press the "Search" tab at the bottom, type the app's name, keywords, or category in the search field, and hit "Search."

Select the App: When you identify the app you want to install, press on its icon or name to view its information page.

Download the App:

On the app's details page, touch the "Get" button (or the app's pricing, if it's a paid app).

If asked, use Face ID, Touch ID, or your Apple ID password to authenticate the download.

Wait for Installation: The app will begin downloading and installing on your device. The app's icon will display on your Home Screen after it's installed.

Access the App: Tap the app's icon on your Home Screen to open and use it.

Updating Apps:

Open the App Store: Launch the App Store from your Home Screen.

Go to the Updates Tab: At the bottom of the App Store, touch the "Updates" tab to browse available app updates. **Update All Apps:**

To update all applications at once, touch "Update All" at the top of the screen.

You may need to verify with Face ID, Touch ID, or your Apple ID password to confirm the upgrades.

Update Individual Apps:

If you wish to update particular applications, browse through the list of available updates and touch "Update" next to each app you want to update.

Wait for Updates: The chosen applications will download and install their updates. You can follow the development on the Updates tab.

Open Updated Apps: After an update is installed, the updated app will still be available from your Home Screen as normal.

Automatic Updates (Optional):

You may activate automatic app upgrades by navigating to "Settings" > "App Store."

Toggle on "App Updates" to enable your iPhone to automatically update applications in the background when new versions are available.

By following these instructions, you may simply install new applications and keep your old apps up to date on your iPhone 15. Regularly upgrading your programs ensures that you get the newest features, bug fixes, and security updates.

Media and Entertainment

Your iPhone 15 is a flexible gadget for enjoying many sorts of media and leisure. From streaming films to listening to music and playing games, here's how to get the most of your iPhone's entertainment features:

Streaming Video and Movies:

Apple TV: Access the Apple TV app to view movies, TV series, and Apple Originals. You may also subscribe to streaming services like Apple TV.

Third-Party applications: Download popular streaming applications like Netflix, Amazon Prime Video, Disney+, Hulu, and YouTube to watch a broad choice of content.

Music and Podcasts:

Apple Music: Subscribe to Apple Music for a wide selection of music and playlists. Create your music collection and discover new songs.

Podcasts: Use the Podcasts app to listen to podcasts on different themes. Subscribe to your favorite programs and download episodes for offline listening.

Gaming:

App Store Games: Explore a large range of mobile games on the App Store. Download and play games ranging from easy puzzles to deep RPGs.

Apple Arcade: Consider subscribing to Apple Arcade for access to a premium library of ad-free games.

Ebooks and Audiobooks:

Apple Books: Use the Apple Books app to buy and read ebooks or listen to audiobooks. The program also supports PDFs.

News and Magazines:

Apple News: Access news stories from many sources and subscribe to premium news magazines for in-depth coverage.

Apple News (Availability varies by region): Subscribe to Apple News+ for access to a broad choice of periodicals and premium content.

TV and Video Streaming to Other Devices:

AirPlay: Stream video and music material from your iPhone to compatible Apple TV, smart TVs, and speakers with AirPlay.

Camera and Photography:

Camera App: Capture and edit images and movies on your iPhone 15. Explore photography applications for sophisticated editing and artistic effects.

AR and VR Experiences:

AR applications: Try augmented reality (AR) applications for interactive experiences and games.

VR applications: Some VR applications and experiences are available for usage with compatible headsets.

Accessibility Features:

Accessibility: The iPhone includes several accessibility features to improve the entertainment experience for individuals with impairments.

Screen Time and Parental Controls:

Screen Time: Monitor and impose restrictions on screen time to preserve a healthy balance between entertainment and other pursuits.

Parental Controls: Use parental control options to block access to particular applications and material for minors.

Your iPhone 15 is a portable entertainment center that can appeal to varied preferences and interests. Whether you're enjoying your favorite TV programs, playing games, or discovering new music, you have a world of entertainment at your fingertips.

Taking and Editing Photos

Taking and editing images on your iPhone 15 is a joyful experience, owing to its enhanced camera capabilities and excellent editing tools. Here's how to capture and improve your photos:

Taking Photos:

Open the Camera App: Locate the Camera app on your Home Screen or swipe right from the Lock Screen to access the camera fast.

Choose a Camera Mode: Swipe left or right to choose between camera settings including Photo, Portrait, Night, and more. Use the zoom slider or pinch motions to modify the zoom level.

Concentrate and Exposure: Tap on the screen where you wish to concentrate. The camera will adjust the exposure and focus appropriately. Swipe up or down on the screen to manually adjust exposure.

Take a picture: Tap the shutter button (the circle) to shoot a picture. Alternatively, use the volume buttons or the volume button on your linked headphones to snap a picture.

Live Photos (Optional): If enabled, Live Photos record a few seconds of video along with the snapshot. You may press and hold the picture to watch it come to life.

Portrait Mode (Optional): In Portrait mode, the iPhone provides a depth effect, blurring the backdrop to let the subject stand out.

Editing Photos:

Open the Photos App: Locate the Photos app on your Home Screen.

Select a picture: Tap on the picture you wish to modify to open it.

Tap "Edit" (top right corner): This will bring up the editing tools.

Basic Editing: You may edit exposure, brightness, contrast, and color by touching the adjustment sliders.

Crop and Rotate: Tap the crop symbol to crop the picture or use the rotate button to straighten it.

Filters: Apply numerous filters to modify the atmosphere and style of your shot.

Portrait Mode Effects (If applicable): For images shot in Portrait mode, you may alter the background blur

(bokeh) and lighting effects.

Undo and Redo: If you make a mistake, press the undo arrow, or if you wish to restore an undo, hit the redo arrow.

Save Your Edits: After editing, hit "Done" to save your changes.

Duplicate the Photo: If you wish to preserve the original and altered versions, press "Duplicate" before saving.

Revert to Original: At any point, you may press "Revert" to delete your adjustments and return to the original picture.

Share Your altered picture: Tap the share button to email your altered picture to friends or publish it on social media.

Third-Party Editing Programs: For more sophisticated editing, try installing third-party photo editing programs like Adobe Lightroom, VSCO, or Snapseed from the App Store. These programs provide a broad variety of creative editing tools and filters.

With your iPhone 15's camera and editing capabilities, you can snap breathtaking photographs and tweak them to your taste, turning your smartphone into a powerful instrument for photography and creative expression.

Music and Podcasts

Music:

Apple Music: Apple Music is a subscription-based music streaming service featuring a massive collection of songs and playlists. Subscribe to Apple Music using the Music app or through the App Store if it's not pre-installed on your device. Explore curated playlists, make your playlists, and discover new music.

Music Library: The Music app also helps you to organize your music library, including tracks you've bought, imported, or synced from your computer.

Listening to Music: Open the Music app and hit "Library" to access your music. Use the "Search" option to search certain songs, albums, or artists. Tap the "Browse" option to find new songs and playlists.

Playlists and Radio: Create and manage playlists to group music together. Access Apple Music Radio for tailored radio stations and programs.

Offline Listening: You can download music and playlists for offline listening when you don't have an internet connection.

Podcasts:

Podcasts App: The Podcasts app is pre-installed on your iPhone 15 and is your entrance to a world of audio material.

Discovering Podcasts: Explore the "Listen Now," "Browse," and "Library" options to locate podcasts. Search for particular podcasts by name or subject.

Subscribing and Downloading: Subscribe to your favorite podcasts to get new episodes automatically.

Download episodes for offline listening.

Listening and Managing: Tap on a podcast to browse episodes and start listening. You may modify the playback speed and skip ahead or backward. Organize your podcasts into playlists and libraries.

Apple Podcasts Subscriptions (Optional): Apple provides a subscription option for select podcasts that may feature ad-free listening and unique content.

Podcast Recommendations: The app may recommend podcasts depending on your listening history.

Whether you're a music aficionado or a podcast lover, the iPhone 15 delivers a simple and engaging experience for finding, listening to, and managing your audio material. Explore and make the most of the Music and Podcasts applications to enrich your pleasure on the move.

Music Playback and Library

Music Playback:

launch the Music App: Locate the Music app on your Home Screen, and press it to launch.

Access Your Music Library: Tap "Library" at the bottom to access your music library.

Playlists: You may browse and play your playlists by touching the "Playlists" section. To make a new playlist, hit the "+" icon and give it a name. To play a playlist, touch its title, and then tap a song to start playing.

Albums: The "Albums" section lists all your albums. Tap on an album to view its tracklist and play songs. Tap the album cover image to see a bigger view with playing options.

Artists: The "Artists" section arranges your music by artists. Tap an artist's name to view their albums and songs. Tap a song to start playing it.

Songs: The "Songs" section contains all your songs in alphabetical order. Scroll through the list to locate and play a certain song.

Search for Music: Use the "Search" option at the bottom to search for particular songs, albums, artists, or playlists.

Now Playing Screen: When playing a song, press the bar at the bottom of the screen to enter the "Now Playing" screen, where you can control playback, change volume, and check song details.

Playback Controls: On the "Now Playing" screen, you may pause, skip, rewind, or shuffle music using the playback controls.

Managing Your Music Library:

Adding Music: To add music to your library, you may buy songs from the iTunes Store, download them from the Apple Music catalog, or import music from your computer using iTunes.

Creating Playlists: Create playlists to arrange your favorite tunes. To create a new playlist, hit the "+" button in the "Playlists" section.

Downloading Music: For offline listening, hit the download button (cloud with arrow) next to a song, album, or playlist to download it to your device.

Deleting Music: To remove a song from your smartphone but retain it in your library, swipe left on the song in the list and select "Remove." To delete a song from your library altogether, go to the song's information page and hit the three dots (ellipsis) symbol, then pick

"Delete from Library."

Syncing Music from Computer: If you have a music collection on your computer, you can sync it with your iPhone using iTunes or the Apple Music app on macOS

Catalina and later.

Apple Music Library: If you subscribe to Apple Music, you may access a wide library of music and albums and add them to your collection. You are able to download or stream these songs.

Your iPhone 15 features a rich music listening experience and library management capabilities, enabling you to enjoy your favorite songs wherever you go. Whether you like playlists, albums, or individual songs, your music collection is at your fingertips.

Podcasts and Streaming Services

Podcasts:

Open the Podcasts App: Find and tap the Podcasts app on your Home Screen, which has a symbol that looks like a purple microphone.

Discovering Podcasts: On the "Listen Now" tab, you'll see a mix of episodes from your subscribed podcasts and tailored suggestions. Explore the "Browse" option to find new podcasts by genre, charts, and collections. Use the "Search" option to search particular podcasts by name or subject.

Subscribing to Podcasts: To subscribe to a podcast, touch on its symbol or name to visit the podcast's information page. Tap the "Subscribe" button to get new episodes automatically. Subscribed podcasts are displayed in the "Library" under "Shows."

Listening to Podcasts: Tap on a podcast to watch its episodes. Tap an episode to start listening. You may modify the playback speed and skip ahead or backward. Download episodes for offline listening by touching the cloud symbol next to an episode.

Managing Podcasts: Organize your podcasts into playlists and libraries. Create personalized playlists by pressing the "Add Playlist" option in the "Library."

Apple Podcasts Subscriptions (Optional): Some podcasts provide premium material via Apple Podcasts

Subscriptions, which might include ad-free listening and unique episodes.

Streaming Services (Apple Music and Others):

Apple Music: Apple Music is Apple's subscription-based music streaming service. You may subscribe to it using the Music app. Search for songs, albums, or artists, and stream them on-demand. Make playlists and download music to listen to offline.

Other Streaming Services: You may also utilize other music streaming services like Spotify, Amazon Music, or Tidal by installing their applications from the App Store. Most of these sites provide free and premium membership alternatives with extra functionality.

Listening to Music: Open the Music app (Apple Music) or the app of your selected streaming provider. Search for music, explore playlists, and create your own. Stream music via Wi-Fi or cellular connection (data costs may apply) or download tracks for offline listening.

Playlists & Offline Listening: Create playlists with your favorite music and share them with others. Download songs for offline listening when you don't have an internet connection.

Radio and Discovery: Many streaming services include custom radio stations and music discovery capabilities to help you find new music.

Subscription Management: Manage your subscription, payment, and account settings using the corresponding app for your streaming provider.

Integration with Apple Music: Apple Music may be combined with your iTunes collection and the Music app for a smooth music listening experience.

Whether you like podcasts or music streaming, the iPhone 15 gives a broad selection of alternatives to consume audio material on the move. Explore, subscribe, and build playlists to customize your entertainment experience to your interests.

Advanced Features

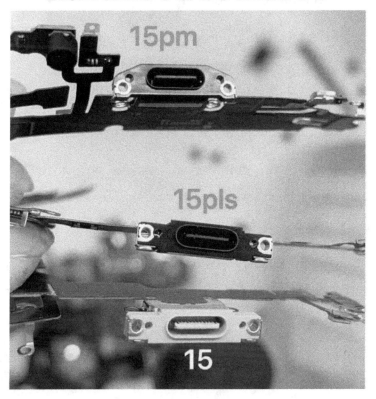

Advanced features on your iPhone 15 increase its usefulness and give extra possibilities beyond the basics. Here are some advanced features to explore:

Face ID and Touch ID: Securely unlock your smartphone and authenticate with applications and services using Face ID (facial recognition) or Touch ID (fingerprint recognition).

Siri Shortcuts: Create custom voice-activated shortcuts to automate chores and control applications with Siri.

Apple Pay: Make safe payments in shops, apps, and online with Apple Pay, connected to your credit or debit cards.

Widgets: Customize your Home Screen with widgets that deliver at-a-glance information from your favorite applications.

Multitasking: Use multitasking gestures to move between programs and launch several apps in split-screen or slide-over view on iPad devices.

AssistiveTouch: Enable AssistiveTouch for configurable on-screen touch controls, helpful for accessibility and rapid access to activities.

VoiceOver: Activate VoiceOver, Apple's screen-reading capability, to aid individuals with visual impairments in managing the iPhone.

Guided Access: Use Guided Access to confine the device to a single app and control which capabilities are accessible inside that app.

VPN and Private surfing: Configure a Virtual Private Network (VPN) for greater privacy and security when surfing the internet. Use Safari's Private Browsing mode to surf the web without storing history or cookies.

Apple CarPlay: Connect your iPhone to a compatible car's infotainment system to access navigation, music, messages, and more while driving.

AirPlay: Stream music and video from your iPhone to AirPlay-enabled devices like Apple TV, smart TVs, and speakers.

Do Not Disturb: Customize Do Not Disturb settings to mute calls, alerts, and messages at particular periods or while you're using certain apps.

Screen Time: Monitor and control your screen time, establish app limitations, and monitor device use habits.

Augmented Reality (AR): Explore AR applications and games that utilize the iPhone's camera and sensors to create interactive experiences.

External Devices: Connect numerous external devices and peripherals, like headphones, gaming controllers, and more, to increase your iPhone's capabilities.

Shortcuts Automation: Create automated routines using the Shortcuts app to initiate tasks depending on time, location, or other factors.

Low Power Mode: Enable Low Power Mode to save energy life when your device's battery is going low.

Screen Recording: Record your iPhone's screen and audio to make lessons, and demonstrations, or share your screen with others.

5G Connectivity (if available): Take advantage of better 5G network speeds for quicker downloads, smoother streaming, and enhanced online experiences.

Advanced Camera Features: Explore advanced camera features like ProRAW and ProRes video recording (available on certain iPhone models).

These sophisticated features may help you get the most out of your iPhone 15 and adapt your smartphone to your requirements and tastes. Take the time to investigate and customize these features to improve your user experience.

Security and Privacy

Ensuring the security and privacy of your iPhone 15 is vital to secure your personal information and preserve control over your data. Here are some suggestions and features to increase your device's security and privacy:

Passcode, Face ID, or Touch ID: Set a strong passcode, activate Face ID (if available), or utilize Touch ID for device authentication.

Two-Factor Authentication (2FA): Enable 2FA for your Apple ID and other online accounts to provide an additional degree of protection.

Automatic Updates: Keep your smartphone up-to-date by activating automatic iOS updates in "Settings" >

"Software Update."

App Permissions: Review and adjust app permissions in "Settings" > "Privacy" to restrict what data applications may access.

App monitoring Transparency (ATT): In iOS 14.5 and later, applications are obliged to obtain your permission before monitoring your activities across other apps and websites. Consider activating this feature.

Strong, Unique Passwords: Use a password manager to create and store complicated, unique passwords for your accounts.

FaceTime and Messaging Security: Use end-to-end encryption for FaceTime and iMessage communications, ensuring your messages and calls stay private.

Find My iPhone: Enable "Find My" under "Settings" > "Your Name" > "Find My" to find and remotely erase your device if it's lost or stolen.

Safari Privacy Features: Use Safari's Intelligent Tracking Prevention to prevent cross-site tracking cookies. Consider activating "Prevent Cross-Site Tracking" and "Block All Cookies" for improved privacy.

Location Services: Manage app access to your location under "Settings" > "Privacy" > "Location Services." Choose "While Using the App" for applications that require location data.

App Store Privacy Labels: Pay attention to privacy labels on programs in the App Store to learn how they manage your data.

VPN (Virtual Private Network): Consider utilizing a trustworthy VPN provider for added privacy while surfing the internet.

Screen Lock Timeout: Set your device to automatically lock after a brief period of inactivity.

Emergency SOS: Configure Emergency SOS settings to swiftly call for assistance in crises.

App Store Downloads: Only download programs from the official App Store to avoid the risk of viruses or compromised apps.

Data Encryption: iOS devices are encrypted by default. Ensure that your smartphone is passcode-protected to keep your data secure.

Limit Ad following: In "Settings" > "Privacy" > "Advertising," activate "Limit Ad Tracking" to stop advertisers from following your device.

Third-Party applications: Review the privacy policies of third-party applications before downloading them and be careful about allowing unneeded rights.

Remove Data After unsuccessful tries: Enable "Erase

You can choose to erase your device's data after a predetermined number of failed passcodes attempts by going to "Settings" > "Face ID & Passcode" (or "Touch ID & Passcode").

Privacy Report (Safari): Use Safari's Privacy Report to check how websites monitor your surfing activities.

By applying these security and privacy precautions, you can guarantee that your iPhone 15 stays a secure and private device, keeping your personal information from illegal access and securing your online activity.

Face ID with Passcode

Face ID and passcode are security features on your iPhone 15 that assist in securing your smartphone and the data saved on it. Here's how they function and how to put them up:

Face ID: Face ID is a face recognition technology that enables you to unlock your iPhone, make secure payments, and access other applications and services by merely glancing at your smartphone.

Setting Up Face ID:

Go to "Settings" on your iPhone.

Scroll down and touch on "Face ID & Passcode."

Enter your device passcode to access Face ID settings.

Tap "Set Up Face ID."

Position your face inside the on-screen frame, and your iPhone will scan your face. Move your head in a circle to finish the scan.

Once the setup is complete, hit "Continue."

You may select whether to activate Face ID for unlocking your iPhone, making payments, or other services.

Using Face ID: To unlock your iPhone, just wake it up (by pressing the screen or raising it) and gaze at your device. For secure app and payment verification, Face ID will urge you to gaze at your smartphone.

Passcode: A passcode is a number or alphanumeric code that acts as an extra layer of protection for your iPhone. You may use it in combination with Face ID or Touch ID or as the main means of unlocking your smartphone.

Setting Up or Changing a Passcode:

Go to "Settings."

Simply touch "Face ID & Passcode" after swiping down. (or

"Touch ID & Passcode" if you're using an earlier iPhone).

Enter your existing passcode.

Scroll down and touch "alter Passcode" to set up a new passcode or alter your old one.

Using a Passcode: When Face ID fails to identify your face or if you restart your device, you'll be requested to enter your passcode to unlock your iPhone. You may also use your password for app and payment verification if you choose not to depend on biometric measures.

Security Tips:

Ensure your passcode is strong and not readily guessable.

Do not reveal your passcode or allow others to see it as you enter it.

Regularly change your passcode for enhanced security.

By setting up Face ID and having a secure password, you can safeguard your iPhone and the critical information it carries from illegal access. These security features assist in guaranteeing that your device stays private and safe.

Privacy Settings and App Permissions

Protecting your privacy on your iPhone 15 entails maintaining privacy settings and app permissions. Here's how to manage what information applications may access:

Privacy Settings:

Open Settings: Tap the "Settings" app on your Home

Screen.

Scroll Down: Scroll down and seek for the "Privacy" option. Tap it to see different privacy options.

Location Services: Tap "Location Services" to manage which applications may access your location. You may select to grant access "Always," "While Using the App," or "Never."

Contacts, Calendars, Reminders, and Photos: Under "Privacy," you'll discover choices like "Contacts," "Calendars," "Reminders," and "Photos." Tap these options to see which applications have requested access to these data categories and alter permissions appropriately.

Microphone and Camera: Control which applications may access your microphone and camera under the corresponding settings. You may allow or prohibit access as required.

Health and Fitness: Manage app access to your health and fitness data under the "Health" area. Review and adjust permissions for particular applications.

HomeKit: In the "Privacy" area, you can also locate "HomeKit." Here, you can control which applications have access to your HomeKit accessories and data.

Bluetooth: Some applications may seek access to

Bluetooth. Control Bluetooth permissions under "Settings" > "Privacy" > "Bluetooth."

Media & Apple Music: Control which applications may access your media collection and Apple Music data.

App Permissions:

App Permissions During Installation:

When you install a new app, it may request access to several data kinds, such as location, contacts, or photographs. You'll be requested to give or refuse certain permissions during installation.

Review App Permissions: To review or adjust app permissions for existing apps: Go to "Settings" > "Privacy."

Choose the applicable category (e.g., Location Services, Contacts).

You'll see a list of applications with their permission settings.

Tap on an app to alter its access level.

Location Services: For location permissions, you may select to grant access "Always," "While Using the App," or "Never" for each app.

Reset App Permissions: If you wish to reset all app permissions to their default settings, you may do so under "Settings" > "General" > "Reset" > "Reset Location & Privacy."

Update for background apps: You may manage which apps are able to update data in the background by going to "Settings" > "General" > "Background App Refresh."

This may affect both privacy and battery life.

App monitoring Transparency (ATT): In iOS 14.5 and later, applications are obliged to obtain permission before monitoring their activities across other apps and websites. You may set or disable this function under "Settings" > "Privacy" > "Tracking."

Limit Ad following: In "Settings" > "Privacy" > "Advertising," activate "Limit Ad Tracking" to stop advertisers from following your device.

By changing privacy settings and app permissions, you may have greater control over your data and safeguard your privacy while still enjoying the functionality of your favorite applications. Review these settings frequently to guarantee your privacy choices are preserved.

Troubleshooting and FAQs

Here are some typical troubleshooting hints and frequently asked questions (FAQs) for iPhone users:

My iPhone Won't Turn On:

Check whether the battery is charged or try a different charger and cord.

Perform a forced restart by swiftly pushing and releasing the Volume Up button, followed by the Volume Down button, and then holding the Side button until you see the Apple logo.

My iPhone is Frozen or Not Responding:

Force reset your iPhone (as indicated above) to alleviate unresponsiveness.

If an app is producing trouble, consider dismissing it by swiping it off the app switcher or removing and reinstalling the program.

No Sound or Low Volume:

Ensure that the volume is cranked up using the actual volume buttons.

Check whether the quiet mode switch on the side of the iPhone is turned off.

Clean the speaker and check there's no dirt obstructing it. **Poor Battery Life:**

Review your energy use in "Settings" > "energy" to detect power-hungry applications.

Adjust settings like screen brightness, background app refresh, and push email to preserve power.

Consider changing the battery if it's considerably deteriorated.

No Cellular or Wi-Fi Connection:

To reset connections, switch Airplane Mode on and off.

Restart your router or modem for Wi-Fi difficulties.

Check whether there's a carrier or Wi-Fi signal in the vicinity.

Reset network settings under "Settings" > "General" >

"Reset" > "Reset Network Settings."

Apps Crashing or Not Working:

Update the app to the newest version from the App

Store.

Restart your iPhone to resolve temporary issues.

Check for iOS updates under "Settings" > "General" >

"Software Update."

Not Receiving Text Messages or iMessages:

Make sure you have a stable cellular or Wi-Fi connection.

Check whether you've banned the sender mistakenly in the Messages app.

Verify that the sender has the right phone number or email address for you.

Forgotten Passcode: If you forget your passcode and don't have access to Face ID or Touch ID, you may need to restore your device using iTunes or Finder on a computer.

Overheating:

Avoid exposing your iPhone to high temperatures.

Close background programs and adjust screen brightness to minimize overheating after heavy use.

Photos Not Syncing to iCloud:

Ensure iCloud Photos is enabled in "Settings" > [Your Name] > "iCloud" > "Photos."

Check your iCloud storage to ensure there's adequate space for photographs.

Can I Use a Different Charger or Cable?

- Yes, you may use third-party chargers and cords, however, it's encouraged to use Apple-certified accessories to prevent any compatibility or safety concerns.

How Do I Backup My iPhone?

- Use iCloud Backup or iTunes/Finder on your PC to generate frequent backups of your iPhone's data.

How Do I Take a Screenshot?

- Press the Side button and Volume Up button simultaneously to snap a screenshot.

How Can I End Background-Running Apps? - On iPhone X or later, slide up from the bottom and stop in the center to open the app switcher. Swipe the app windows up to close them.

How Do I Enable Dark Mode?

- You may activate Dark Mode under "Settings" > "Display & Brightness." Choose the "Dark" look.

How Do I Enable Low Power Mode?

- You may activate Low Power Mode in "parameters" > "Battery." It minimizes power usage by altering several parameters.

If you experience particular difficulties not addressed here, feel free to ask for more thorough troubleshooting procedures. Additionally, you may call Apple Support or visit an Apple Store for assistance with more difficult issues.

Accessories and Tips

Accessories:

iPhone cover: Protect your iPhone 15 from drops and scratches with a sturdy cover. You may select from many designs, including sleek, robust, and pocketbook cases.

Screen Protector: Apply a high-quality screen protector to preserve your iPhone's display free from scratches and mild accidents.

Wireless Charger: Invest in a Qi-compatible wireless charger for quick and cable-free charging.

Portable Power Bank: Carry a portable power bank to guarantee your iPhone has additional battery life while you're on the road.

Bluetooth Headphones or Earbuds: Enjoy cordless audio with Bluetooth headphones or earbuds, excellent for music, calls, and workouts.

External Lens Attachments: Enhance your iPhone's photographic skills with external lens attachments, such as wide-angle and macro lenses.

Apple Watch: Pair your iPhone with an Apple Watch for fitness monitoring, alerts, and simple management of your device.

Smart Keyboard: If you have an iPad model, consider a compatible Smart Keyboard for quick typing and efficiency.

Game Controllers: If you like mobile gaming, utilize a suitable game controller for a better gaming experience.

Tips:

Face ID and Passcode: Set up Face ID with a secure passcode to safeguard your smartphone and data.

iCloud Backup: Enable iCloud Backup to periodically back up your iPhone's data. You can access "Settings" > to do this. > "iCloud" > "iCloud" > [Your Name] Backup."

Widgets: Customize your Home Screen with widgets for easy access to information from your favorite applications.

App Library: Utilize the App Library to organize and easily discover your applications. Swipe right on your last Home Screen page to access it.

App Library Categories: You can also create custom categories in the App Library by dragging and dropping applications into them.

Customize Control Center: Tailor your Control Center by adding or rearranging shortcuts for fast access to settings and functionalities.

Siri Shortcuts: Create custom Siri Shortcuts to automate chores and simplify your everyday routines.

Focus Mode: Use Focus mode to filter alerts depending on your current activity or location. Customize it under

"Settings" > "Focus."

Scheduled Dark Mode: Schedule DarkMode to activate automatically at particular times of the day in "Settings" > "Display & Brightness."

Privacy Features: Review and manage app permissions in "Settings" > "Privacy" to control what data apps can access.

Shortcuts App: Explore the Shortcuts app to develop and utilize automation routines for different activities.

Background App Refresh: Manage which programs can update information in the background to save battery life by going to "Settings" > "General" > "Background App Refresh."

Reduce Motion: If you prefer a less dynamic interface, activate

"Reduce Motion" under "Settings" >

"Accessibility" > "Motion."

Dynamic Wallpapers: Customize your Home Screen with dynamic wallpapers that vary depending on the time of day or your device's light and dark settings.

Keyboard Shortcuts: Learn keyboard shortcuts for text editing, navigation, and more by utilizing motions and keyboard accessories.

Smart Invert Colors: Enable "Smart Invert" in the "Accessibility" options for a dark mode-like look in programs that don't support it.

One-Handed Mode: Activate one-handed mode by double-tapping (not pushing) the Home button or swiping down on the bottom of the screen.

By utilizing these accessories and recommendations, you may enhance the usefulness of your iPhone 15 and modify it to meet your tastes and requirements.

iPhone Accessories

There are several accessories available for your iPhone 15 that may boost its performance and convenience. Here's a list of some popular iPhone accessories:

Phone covers: Protect your iPhone from drops and scratches with a broad choice of phone covers, including thin cases, robust cases, and elegant designs.

Screen Protectors: Apply a screen protector to secure your iPhone's display from scratches and mild accidents.

Wireless Chargers: Qi-compatible wireless chargers enable you to charge your iPhone wirelessly, enabling convenience and eliminating cord clutter.

Portable Chargers (juice Banks): Carry a portable charger to guarantee your iPhone has additional juice while you're on the road.

Lightning cords: Keep extra Lightning cords for charging and data transmission, or select strong braided cables for a lifetime.

Vehicle Mounts and Holders: Use vehicle mounts and holders to secure your iPhone while driving for navigation and hands-free calling.

Headphones & Earbuds: Choose from wired or wireless headphones, earbuds, and over-ear headphones for music, calls, and auditory pleasure.

Bluetooth Speakers: Portable Bluetooth speakers deliver high-quality sound for listening to music or podcasts on the move.

Stylus Pens: For iPhone models with stylus

compatibility, consider using a stylus pen for accurate input and sketching.

Selfie Sticks and Tripods: Capture better images and films with selfie sticks and tripods for steady shoots.

Extra Lenses: Attach extra lenses to your iPhone's camera to improve your pictures, adding fisheye, wide-angle, or macro capabilities.

External Storage: Expand your iPhone's storage capacity with external storage devices that connect by Lightning or wireless choices.

Apple Watch: If you have an Apple Watch, link it with your iPhone for enhanced features, such as fitness monitoring and alerts.

Smart Battery Cases: Apple's smart battery cases give more battery life and protection for your iPhone.

Fitness Accessories: Accessories like fitness bands and heart rate monitors may connect with your iPhone to track your health and fitness statistics.

Gaming Controllers: Game controllers intended for iOS devices increase your gaming experience for compatible games.

Docking Stations: Docking stations can charge and sync your iPhone while providing a comfortable stand for your smartphone.

AR/VR Headsets: Explore augmented reality (AR) and virtual reality (VR) experiences with compatible headsets.

Magnetic Mounts: Magnetic mounts and accessories enable you to connect your iPhone to different surfaces securely.

Protective Films: Besides screen protectors, consider protective films for the back and sides of your iPhone to avoid scratches.

When purchasing accessories for your iPhone 15, check sure they are compatible with your exact model and iOS version. These accessories may increase your iPhone's capabilities, safeguard your device, and make it even more adaptable for numerous jobs and activities.

updates to cameras

A 48-megapixel main camera with an f/1.6 aperture and a 12-megapixel ultra-wide camera with an f/2.4 aperture will both be available on the iPhone 15 and iPhone 15 Plus. There will be no changes to the Ultra Wide lens, but the Main camera will include a brand-new Sony image sensor, which is an enhancement over the sensor found in the iPhone 14 Pro versions.

Cases and Chargers

Cases:

Slim Cases:

Slim cases provide modest protection while keeping the iPhone's thin form.

They are lightweight and offer scratch and small drop protection.

Ideal for people who appreciate a minimalist appearance and feel.

Rugged Cases:

Rugged cases offer powerful protection against drops, shocks, and collisions.

They frequently feature reinforced corners and extra layers of protection.

Perfect for people who work in outdoor locations or have an active lifestyle.

Wallet Cases:

Wallet cases combine phone security with storage for cards, cash, or IDs.

They may replace your wallet, delivering convenience and safety in one.

Great for individuals who wish to travel light.

Clear Cases:

Clear covers display the iPhone's design while offering minimal protection.

They are great for consumers who wish to exhibit the iPhone's elegance.

Some transparent cases contain anti-yellowing technology to retain clarity over time.

Leather Cases:

Leather cases give a luxurious appearance and feel while safeguarding your iPhone.

They acquire a particular patina over time, providing character.

A superb alternative for those who love elegance and endurance.

Silicone Cases:

Silicone cases give a soft, gripping feel for improved grasp.

They provide good drop protection and are pleasant to grip.

Suitable for users who prefer a balance between protection and comfort.

Battery Cases:

Battery covers have an inbuilt battery, prolonging your iPhone's battery life.

They are perfect for heavy users or when you're away from a charger for a lengthy time.

Designer Cases:

Designer cases contain distinctive patterns, artwork, or branding.

A wonderful alternative for people who want their iPhone to stand out.

Chargers:

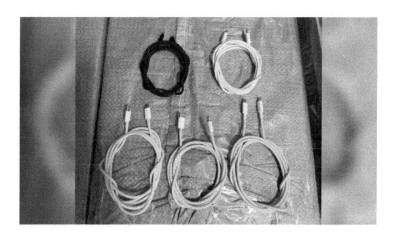

Wireless Chargers:

Qi-compatible wireless chargers enable you to charge your iPhone wirelessly.

They enhance ease and eliminate cable clutter.

Fast Charging Adapters:

Invest in a high-quality USB-C power converter to allow rapid charging for your iPhone.

Apple's 20W USB-C Power Adapter is a popular option.

MagSafe Chargers:

MagSafe chargers employ magnets to align and charge your iPhone wirelessly.

They are compatible with MagSafe-compatible cases and accessories.

Car Chargers:

Car chargers with USB ports or wireless charging capabilities keep your iPhone fueled while on the go.

Some versions feature rapid charging for speedier refilling.

Portable Power Banks:

Portable power banks give an additional battery source while you're away from outlets.

Choose a high-capacity power bank for numerous charges on the fly.

Multi-Port Chargers:

Multi-port chargers enable you to charge numerous devices concurrently.

They are excellent for charging your iPhone together with other electronics.

Solar Chargers:

Solar chargers utilize sunshine to charge your iPhone, making them great for outdoor activities.

Consider versions with built-in batteries for storage.

Car Mount Chargers:

Car mount chargers keep your iPhone secure while charging it throughout your commute.

They are helpful for navigation and hands-free calling.

When purchasing cases and chargers for your iPhone 15, confirm compatibility with your smartphone and consider your use habits and preferences. High-quality accessories not only safeguard your iPhone but also increase your entire user experience.

Tips and Tricks

Face ID Awareness: Face ID works even while you're wearing sunglasses or a hat, but it's a good idea to set up an "Alternate look" under Face ID settings if you use items that dramatically affect your look.

Quick Access to Camera: Swipe left on the Lock Screen or click the Camera symbol on the Lock Screen to swiftly activate the Camera app.

Scan Documents and Photographs: Use the built-in Notes app to scan documents and photographs by making a new note and pressing the camera icon.

Rear Tap: Enable "Back Tap" in "Settings" >

"Accessibility" > "Touch" to conduct activities by double or triple touching the rear of your iPhone.

Custom Widgets: Customize your Home Screen with widgets by long-pressing on the Home Screen, hitting the "+" button, and choosing widgets to add.

Privacy Report in Safari: In Safari, hit the "AA" symbol in the address bar and pick "Privacy Report" to examine how websites monitor your surfing history.

Multilingual Keyboard: You may enable a multilingual keyboard to type in several languages without switching keyboards. Go to "Settings" > "General" > "Keyboard" > "Keyboards" to add languages.

Guided Access: Use Guided Access in "Settings" > "Accessibility" to lock your iPhone within a single app and limit access to particular functions. Great for youngsters or concentrate mode.

Swipe Text Input: When using the normal keyboard, swipe your finger over the keys to swiftly text without raising your finger. Enable this functionality in

"Settings" > "Accessibility" > "Keyboards."

Hidden Magnifier: Activate the Magnifier by

triple-clicking the side button. This function can enlarge text and objects using your iPhone's camera.

Sleep routine: Set a sleep routine in the Health app to monitor your sleep habits and enhance your sleep quality.

Emergency SOS: Quickly call for assistance by pushing and holding the side button and a volume button simultaneously, or by hitting the side button five times fast.

Safari Tab Groups: Organize your open tabs in Safari into tab groups for better navigation.

Offline Reading in Safari: Save web pages for offline reading by touching the share symbol and choosing "Add to Reading List."

Apple ID Recovery Contacts: Set up recovery contacts for your Apple ID under "Settings" > [Your Name] > "Password & Security" > "Account Recovery."

iMessage Effects: Add interesting effects to your iMessage by tapping and holding the send button after entering a message.

Smart Invert Colors: Enable "Smart Invert" in

"Accessibility" options to achieve a dark mode-like look in programs that don't support it natively.

Quick Access to Widgets: Swipe right on your Home Screen to access your widgets for quick information at a glance.

Private Browsing: Open a new Private Browsing tab in Safari to browse without preserving your history or cookies.

iCloud Keychain: Use iCloud Keychain to securely save and autofill passwords across your Apple devices.

These tips and techniques will help you get the most out of your iPhone 15 and enhance your overall user experience. Feel free to explore these features and settings to tailor your smartphone to your tastes.

Hidden Features and Shortcuts

Quick App Switcher: Swipe right on the bottom edge of the screen (near the home indication) to swiftly switch between your recently used applications. This gesture works on iPhone devices without a physical Home button.

Haptic Touch Everywhere: Use Haptic Touch

(long-press) on app icons, links, alerts, and more to obtain fast actions, previews, and extra choices.

Quick go to Top: Tap the top of the screen (the status bar) to swiftly go to the top of a website, program, or document.

Universal Search: Swipe down on the Home Screen to reach the universal search bar, where you can instantly discover applications, contacts, documents, and more.

Undo Typing: Shake your iPhone to undo typing or activities. You may activate this function in "Settings" >

"Accessibility" > "Touch" > "Shake to Undo."

Magnifier: Triple-click the side button to activate the Magnifier, which converts your iPhone into a digital magnifying glass, ideal for reading tiny print or scrutinizing items up close.

Silent Unknown Callers: Enable "mute Unknown Callers" under "Settings" > "Phone" to mute calls from unknown numbers, sending them directly to voicemail.

One-Handed Keyboard: Press and hold the emoji or globe symbol on the keyboard, then pick the left or right one-handed keyboard layout for easier typing with one hand.

Quickly Add a Period: Double-tap the spacebar to add a period and a space at the end of a phrase.

Keyboard Trackpad Mode: On smartphones with 3D Touch, hard-press the keyboard to transform it into a trackpad for accurate text cursor placement.

QR Code Scanner: Use the built-in QR code scanner by launching the Camera app and pointing it at a QR code. A notice will be displayed to guide you to the appropriate material.

Unique App Icons: Create unique app icons with the Shortcuts app to offer your Home Screen a customized appearance.

Emoji Shortcuts: Type a relevant term in Messages or other text fields, and iOS may propose replacing it with an emoji. Tap the word to transform it into an emoji.

Screen Recording in Control Center: Add the Screen

Recording option to Control Center in "Settings" > "Control Center" to simply record your screen.

Safari Reader Mode: Tap the Reader icon in Safari's address bar to see articles in a streamlined, distraction-free manner.

Erase Digits in the Calculator App: If you make a mistake when typing in the Calculator app, swipe left or right on the display to erase the last digit.

Measure App: Use the Measure app to measure things and areas using augmented reality. It's helpful for rapid measurements.

Guided Access Time limitations: When utilizing Guided Access, you may establish time limitations for how long an app can be utilized. Great for controlling screen time.

Bold Text for Accessibility: Enable "Bold Text" in "Settings" > "Display & Brightness" > "Text Size" for more readable text across the system.

Lock Notes with Face ID/Touch ID: Protect sensitive notes by locking them with Face ID or Touch ID in the Notes app.

Appendix

Apple Support: For in-depth troubleshooting, authoritative instructions, and support with your iPhone, visit Apple Support.

Apple Community: Join conversations, ask questions, and share your expertise with other Apple users on the Apple Community.

iOS User Guide: Access the official iOS User Guide by navigating to the "Books" app on your iPhone and searching for "iOS User Guide."

App Store: Explore the App Store to find new applications and updates for your iPhone 15. You may discover applications for numerous reasons, from work to enjoyment.

iTunes and Apple Music: Manage your music, movies, and podcasts with iTunes on your PC and enjoy streaming with Apple Music on your iPhone.

iCloud: Learn more about iCloud and how to manage your iCloud storage and data at iCloud.com.

Apple Developer Documentation: If you're interested in iOS app development or want to delve further into iOS capabilities, check the Apple Developer Documentation.

Third-Party Accessory Manufacturers: Explore trusted third-party accessory manufacturers like Belkin, OtterBox, Anker, and Spigen for a broad choice of iPhone covers, chargers, and accessories.

iOS Upgrades: Keep your iPhone up to date with the newest iOS upgrades by navigating to "Settings" >

"General" > "Software Update."

iOS Tips and Tricks Articles: Various websites and tech blogs give thorough articles about iOS tips, tricks, and hidden features. These may be terrific sources of extra ideas and suggestions.

iOS and iPhone features may change with software upgrades, so it's a good idea to check for the latest information and updates from Apple's official sources.

Glossary of iPhone Terms

iOS: iOS stands for "iPhone Operating System." It's the mobile operating system created by Apple for iPhones, iPads, and iPod Touch devices.

Home Screen: The primary screen on your iPhone where you view app icons and widgets. You can access your applications and features from here.

Lock Screen: The screen that displays when your iPhone is locked. You may check alerts, the time, date, and more from the Lock Screen.

Control Center: A panel that you may reach by swiping down (or up, depending on your device) from the top right corner of the screen. It enables easy access to settings including Wi-Fi, brightness, and more.

Notification Center: A location where you can view all your alerts in one list. Swipe down from the top of the screen to access it.

App Store: Apple's digital marketplace where you may download and install applications for your iPhone.

iCloud: Apple's cloud storage and syncing service. It lets you backup your data, exchange files, and sync material across your Apple devices.

Apple ID: Your Apple ID is your unique identification for utilizing Apple services. You use it to download applications, make purchases, and access iCloud.

Face ID: Apple's facial recognition technology enables you to unlock your iPhone and authenticate transactions and logins using your face.

Touch ID: Apple's fingerprint identification technology that enables you to unlock your iPhone and authenticate transactions and logins using your fingerprint.

Siri: Apple's voice-activated virtual assistant. You can ask Siri questions, create reminders, send messages, and conduct numerous activities.

App Store: Apple's digital marketplace where you may download and install applications and games on your iPhone.

Home Button: A physical button available on previous iPhone models that acted as a primary navigation control. Newer versions employ gesture-based navigation without a Home Button.

FaceTime: Apple's video and audio calling service that enables you to make calls to other Apple devices using a Wi-Fi or cellular connection.

iMessage: Apple's messaging program lets you send text messages, images, videos, and more to other Apple users using Wi-Fi or cellular connections.

AirDrop: A function that enables you to wirelessly exchange photographs, movies, and other data with nearby Apple devices.

Do Not Disturb: A function that silences calls, notifications, and alarms when engaged, beneficial for avoiding disruptions during meetings or when sleeping.

AirPods: Apple's wireless earphones that link to your iPhone through Bluetooth for listening to music, making calls, and utilizing Siri.

Night Mode: A camera function that helps low-light photography by shooting longer exposure photographs to collect more light.

Widgets: Mini-applications that give information and easy access to app functionality on your Home Screen.

5G: The fifth generation of cellular network technology, which enables higher internet rates and enhanced connection when enabled by your carrier and iPhone.

MagSafe: A magnetic technology utilized in recent iPhones for attaching accessories including chargers, cases, and wallets.

App Library: A feature introduced in iOS 14 that organizes your applications automatically and lets you access them from a dedicated screen.

Focus Mode: A feature introduced in iOS 15 that allows you to filter alerts depending on your current activity or location to prevent distractions.

Shortcuts: Automation that enables you to create custom actions or sequences of activities on your iPhone to expedite chores.

These words should help you explore and understand your iPhone's capabilities and operations more efficiently.

www.ingramcontent.com/pod-product-compliance
Lightning Source LLC
LaVergne TN
LVHW051659050326
832903LV00032B/3901